To Sister M. Georgia

from

Christmas 19

The Tears of The Blind Lions

for JACQUES MARITAIN

BY THOMAS MERTON

"When those who love God try to talk about Him, their words are blind lions looking for springs in the desert."
                                        —LÉON BLOY

THOMAS MERTON

THE TEARS

OF THE

BLIND LIONS

NEW DIRECTIONS

ACKNOWLEDGMENT

Some of these poems first appeared in The Atlantic Monthly, The Partisan Review, Horizon, Poetry, The Hudson Review, Spirit, The Month, The Commonweal and Epoch.

Nihil Obstat

JOHN M. A. FEARNS, S.T.D.

CENSOR LIBRORUM

Imprimatur

✠FRANCIS CARDINAL SPELLMAN

ARCHBISHOP OF NEW YORK

Ex Parte Ordinis:

Nihil Obstat

FRATER M. GABRIEL O'CONNELL, O.C.S.O.

FRATER M. ANTHONY CHASSAGNE, O.C.S.O.

Imprimi Potest

FRATER M. DOMINIQUE NOGUES, O.C.S.O.

ABBAS GENERALIS

September 27, 1949

PRINTED IN THE UNITED STATES

BY TURCK AND REINFELD, NEW YORK

New Directions Books are published by James Laughlin

NEW YORK OFFICE — 333 SIXTH AVENUE

Song

When rain, (sings light) rain has devoured my house
And wind wades through my trees,
The cedars fawn upon the storm with their huge paws.
Silence is louder than a cyclone
In the rude door, my shelter.
And there I eat my air alone
With pure and solitary songs

While others sit in conference.
Their windows grieve, and soon frown
And glass begins to wrinkle with a multitude of water
Till I no longer see their speech
And they no longer know my theater.

Rivers clothe their houses
And hide their naked wisdom.
Their conversations
Go down into the deep like submarines:
Submerge them, with their pale expressions, in my storm.

But I drink rain, drink wind
Distinguish poems
Boiling up out of the cold forest:
Lift to the wind my eyes full of water,
My face and mind, to take their free refreshment.

Thus I live on my own land, on my own island
And speak to God, my God, under the doorway
When rain, (sings light) rain has devoured my house
And winds wade through my trees.

Hymn for the Feast of Duns Scotus

On a day in fall, when high winds trouble the country
I visit the borders of my world, and see the colored hills.
And while I walk upon their coasts
The woods and grasses tumble like a sea:
Their waters run after the dry shores
Of the path made for my feet.
And I open the book of Duns Scotus,
To learn the reason for theology.

This is the book whose vision is not its own end,
Whose words are the ways of love, whose term is Trinity:
Three Who is One Who is Love.

One, because One is the reason for loving
And the One Love loved. But Three
Are the Three Lovers Who love and are loved
And are Love.

One is the Love we love, and love for:
But Three are those we love and
One our Three Lovers, loving One another.
Their One Love for One another is their Love for us,
And One is our Love for all Three and all One
And for us, on earth, brothers, one another!

One God is the One Love *propter quam amatur*
And Three Persons of the One Love are *quae amantur*.
So to love One alone is little better
Than loving none.
But to love Three is to love One.

Now today, while these Three
Love One another in me,
Loving me, and I love them,
Suddenly I can no longer live in mortal flesh,

Because your book, O Scotus, burns me like a branding
    iron!
If I could only breathe I would cry out, if I could cry,
To tell someone what Voices robbed me of my being!

For the sound of my Beloved,
The voice of the sound of my Three Beloved
(One of my Three of my One Beloved)
Comes down out of the heavenly depths
And hits my heart like thunder:
And lo! I am alive and dead
With heart held fast in that Three-Personed Love.

And lo! God, my God!
Look! Look! I travel in Thy strength
I swing in the grasp of Thy Love, Thy great Love's One
    Strength,
I run Thy swift ways, Thy straightest rails
Until my life becomes Thy Life and sails or rides like an
    express!

Word, the whole universe swells with Thy wide-open
    speed,
Father, the world bursts, breaks, huge Spirit, with Thy
    might
Then land, sea and wind swing
And roll from my forgotten feet
While God sings victory, sings victory
In the blind day of that defeat.

The Quickening of St. John the Baptist

On the Contemplative Vocation

Why do you fly from the drowned shores of Galilee,
From the sands and the lavender water?
Why do you leave the ordinary world, Virgin of Nazareth,
The yellow fishing boats, the farms,
The winesmelling yards and low cellars
Or the oilpress, and the women by the well?
Why do you fly those markets,
Those suburban gardens,
The trumpets of the jealous lilies,
Leaving them all, lovely among the lemon trees?

You have trusted no town
With the news behind your eyes.
You have drowned Gabriel's word in thoughts like seas
And turned toward the stone mountain
To the treeless places.
Virgin of God, why are your clothes like sails?

The day Our Lady, full of Christ,
Entered the dooryard of her relative
Did not her steps, light steps, lay on the paving leaves
    like gold?
Did not her eyes as grey as doves
Alight like the peace of a new world upon that house,
    upon miraculous Elizabeth?

Her salutation
Sings in the stone valley like a Charterhouse bell:
And the unborn saint John
Wakes in his mother's body,
Bounds with the echoes of discovery.

8

Sing in your cell, small anchorite!
How did you see her in the eyeless dark?
What secret syllable
Woke your young faith to the mad truth
That an unborn baby could be washed in the Spirit of
    God?
Oh burning joy!
What seas of life were planted by that voice!
With what new sense
Did your wise heart receive her Sacrament,
And know her cloistered Christ?

You need no eloquence, wild bairn,
Exulting in your hermitage.
Your ecstasy is your apostolate,
For whom to kick is *contemplata tradere.*
Your joy is the vocation
Of Mother Church's hidden children —
Those who by vow lie buried in the cloister or the
    hermitage:
The speechless Trappist, or the grey, granite Carthusian,
The quiet Carmelite, the barefoot Clare,
Planted in the night of contemplation,
Sealed in the dark and waiting to be born.

Night is our diocese and silence is our ministry
Poverty our charity and helplessness our tongue-tied
    sermon.
Beyond the scope of sight or sound we dwell upon the air
Seeking the world's gain in an unthinkable experience.
We are exiles in the far end of solitude, living as listeners
With hearts attending to the skies we cannot understand:
Waiting upon the first far drums of Christ the
    Conqueror,
Planted like sentinels upon the world's frontier.

But in the days, rare days, when our Theotocos
Flying the prosperous world
Appears upon our mountain with her clothes like sails,
Then, like the wise, wild baby,
The unborn John who could not see a thing
We wake and know the Virgin Presence
Receive her Christ into our night
With stabs of an intelligence as white as lightning.

Cooled in the flame of God's dark fire
Washed in His gladness like a vesture of new flame
We burn like eagles in His invincible awareness
And bound and bounce with happiness,
Leap in the womb, our cloud, our faith, our element,
Our contemplation, our anticipated heaven
Till Mother Church sings like an Evangelist.

The Reader

Lord, when the clock strikes
Telling the time with cold tin
And I sit hooded in this lectern

Waiting for the monks to come,
I see the red cheeses, and bowls
All smile with milk in ranks upon their tables.

Light fills my proper globe
(I have won light to read by
With a little, tinkling chain)

And the monks come down the cloister
With robes as voluble as water.
I do not see them but I hear their waves.

It is winter, and my hands prepare
To turn the pages of the saints:
And to the trees Thy moon has frozen on the windows
My tongue shall sing Thy Scripture.

Then the monks pause upon the step
(With me here in this lectern
And Thee there on Thy crucifix)
And gather little pearls of water on their fingers' ends
Smaller than this my psalm.

From the Legend of St. Clement

I have seen the sun
Spilling its copper petals on the Black Sea
By the base of the prisoners' cliff
Where, from the acts of martyrs,
Tall poems grow up like buildings.

Deep in the wall of the wounded mountain
(Where seas no longer frown)
The songs of the martyrs come up like cities or buildings.
Their chains shine with hymns
And their hands cut down the giant blocks of stone.

Poetry, psalms
Flower with a huge architecture
Raising their grandeur on the gashed cape.
Words of God blaze like a disaster

In the windows of their prophetic cathedral.
But the sighs of the deep multitude
Grow out of the mountain's heart as clean as vines.

O martyrs! O tremendous prisoners!
Burying your murder in this marble hill!
The Lamb shall soon stand
White as a shout against the sky:
His feet shall soon strike rainbows from the rock.
The cliffs give up their buried streams.
Throw down the chains of your wrists, prisoners!
Drink, and swim!

The winds have carried your last sentences
Across Ukraine.
Your poetry shall grow in distant places.
Asia, Greece, Egypt, England know your name.
Your hymns shall stand like vineyards
And swing with fruit in other worlds, in other centuries.

And your ecstasy shall make shade,
Foliage for summers unforeseen
To cover travellers in continents you have not known
When the temples have fallen,
The theaters cemented in your blood have long ago
    fallen.

Your joy echoes across the carved ridge
Plays across mountains
Stands like fleets or islands
Sailing the seas to Greece,
And after twenty times one hundred
Years of repercussion
Your waters shatter the land at my feet with seas forever
    young.

On a Day in August

These woods are too impersonal.
The deaf-and-dumb fields, waiting to be shaved of hay
Suffer the hours like an unexpected sea
While locusts fry their music in the sycamores.

But from the curdled places of the sky
(Where a brown wing hovers for carrion)
We have not seen the heaven-people come.

The clean, white saints, have they forgotten us?
Here we lie upon the earth
In the air of our dead grove
Dreaming some wind may come and kiss ourselves in the
    red eyes
With a pennyworth of mercy for our pepper shoulders.
And so we take into our hands the ruins
Of the words our minds have rent.

It is enough.
Our souls are trying to crawl out of our pores.
Our lives are seeping through each part of us like
    vinegar.
A sad sour death is eating the roots of our hair.

Yet doors of sanitary winds lie open in the clouds
To vistas of those laundries where the clean saints dwell:
If we could only view them from our slum!
But our dream has wandered away
And drowned in the din of the crickets' disconnected
    prayer.

Thus the grasses and the unemployed goldenrod
Go revel through our farm, and dance around the field.
The blue-black lights come shimmering upon the tar
Where kids made footprints in the melting way to
    Louisville.
And spooks come out of the road and walk the jagged heat
Like the time we found that drunkard lying still as
    murder
In the ditch behind the mill.

But you, Saint Clare,
We have been looking up your stairs all afternoon
Wanting to see you walking down some nimbus with
    your gentle friends.

Very well, clouds,
Open your purple bottles,
Cozen us never more with blowsy cotton:
But organize,
Summon the punishing lightning:
Spring those sudden gorgeous trees against the dark
Curtain of apocalypse you'll hang to earth, from heaven:
Let five white branches scourge the land with fire!
And when the first fat drops
Spatter upon the tin top of our church like silver dollars
And thoughts come bathing back to mind with a new life,
Prayer will become our new discovery

When God and His bad earth once more make friends.

14

Christopher Columbus

There was a great Captain with Mary in his sails
Who did not discover Harlem or the East Side
Or Sing Sing or the dead men on the island.
But his heart was like the high mountains.
And when the king gave him money
To go and discover a country
And fixed him up with robes of gold

He threw down all those pesos and stripped to his cham-
 pion skin
And waded into the waters of the sea.
The surf boiled white about his knees
And the tides folded behind him
When he caught the furthest caravels and passed them by.
"There goes Columbus! There he goes!" the sailors cried,
Still he is head and shoulders above the horizon
Leaving us like the pillars of Hercules
Standing westward on the way to the Azores!
What land will he find to believe in, now he knows the
 world is round?

Forest upon forest, mile upon empty mile
The undiscovered continent lies, rock upon rock:
The lakes awake, or move in their mute sleep.
Huge rivers wander where the plains
Are cloudy or dark with seas of buffalo.
Frail waterbirds sing in the weeds of Florida.
Northward, grey seas stir
In sight of the unconscious hills.
There are no prints in the thin snows of Maine.

Suddenly the great Christ-bearing Columbus rises in the
    sea
Spilling the green Atlantic from his shoulders
And sees America through a veil of waters.
Steam things low like cattle all around him in the rivers.
Towers stand like churches on the rock, in a garden of
    boats;
Citizens look up like snap-dragons
Crowding the streets and galleries and saluting heaven
    with their songs.
Music comes cascading down the stones until all walls
Are singing the feasts of the saints in the light of pro-
    cessions.

Then the discoverer, rising from the harbor,
Taking the river in his stride
Overtops all tall palaces.
The people cheer their noon-day sun, their giant Gospel
And calm Columbus reaches down to the citizens
The golden fruits of which his arms are full.

All over the new land woods retire to the hills.
Indians come out of the brake with corn and melons
And he blesses the bronze gentry sitting in the air of the
    arcade:
Thousands of Franciscans go through the fields with
    Sacraments
And towns, towns, towns rise out of the ground.

Then the Americans, wearing the new names of saints
Look up and sing into the face of their tall Father
While he is lifted from the earth, blesses his continent.
Birds fly like language from the cloud, his beard.

His smiles are quickly muffled in the sky.
His gestures mild, they melt and disappear.
Waving, waving the little ones have wept him out of
    sight.

When it is evening, in America's vespers
Feathers of imperfect incense spend themselves
Marking his memory on steeples.
As fast as dark comes down towns, cities,
Returning to the virgin air
Restore these shores to silences.
Woods crawl back into the gulf.
Shadows of Franciscans die in tangled wilds
And there is just one smoke upon the plain
And just one Indian hunter.

What will you do tomorrow, America
Found and lost so soon?
Your Christ has died and gone to Spain
Bearing a precious cross upon his shoulder
And there your story lies in chains.

But the devils are sailing for your harbors
Launching their false doves into the air to fly for your
    sands.
They bend over their tillers with little fox faces,
Grin like dollars through their fur,
And their meat-eating sails fly down and fold upon your
    shore.

Suddenly the silences of the deep continent
Die in a tornado of guitars.
Our own America tears down her mask of trees

Hailing each pirate with sarcastic towns.
Break open a dozen cities! Let traffic bleed upon the land
And hug your hundred and twenty million paupers in a
        vice without escape
While they are mapped and verified
Plotted, printed, catalogued, numbered and categoried
And sold to the doctors of your sham discovery.

*   *   *

And now the cities' eyes are tight as ice
When the long cars stream home in nights of autumn.
(The bells Columbus heard are dumb.)
The city's rivers are as still as liquor.
Bars and factories pool their lights
In Michigan's or Erie's mirrors, now, on the night of the
        game.
(But the bells Columbus heard are dumb.)
The city's face is frozen like a screen of silver
When the universities turn in
And winter sings in the bridges
Tearing the grand harps down.

But the children sing no hymn for the feast of Saint
        Columbus.
They watch the long, long armies drifting home.

St. Malachy

In November, in the days to remember the dead
When air smells cold as earth,
St. Malachy, who is very old, gets up,
Parts the thin curtain of trees and dawns upon our land.

His coat is filled with drops of rain, and he is bearded
With all the seas of Poseidon.
(Is it a crozier, or a trident in his hand?)
He weeps against the gothic window, and the empty
    cloister
Mourns like an ocean shell.

Two bells in the steeple
Talk faintly to the old stranger
And the tower considers his waters.
"I have been sent to see my festival," (his cavern speaks!)
"For I am the saint of the day.
Shall I shake the drops from my locks and stand in your
    transept,
Or, leaving you, rest in the silence of my history?"

So the bells rang and we opened the antiphoners
And the wrens and larks flew up out of the pages.
Our thoughts became lambs. Our hearts swam like seas.
One monk believed that we should sing to him
Some stone-age hymn
Or something in the giant language.
So we played to him in the plainsong of the giant
    Gregory:
Oceans of Scripture sang upon bony Eire.

Then the last salvage of flowers
(Fostered under glass after the gardens foundered)
Held up their little lamps on Malachy's altar
To peer into his wooden eyes before the Mass began.

Rain sighed down the sides of the stone church.
Storms sailed by all day in battle fleets.
At five o'clock, when we tried to see the sun, the speech-
    less visitor
Sighed and arose and shook the humus from his feet
And with his trident stirred our trees
And left down-wood, shaking some drops upon the
    ground.

Thus copper flames fall, tongues of fire fall
The leaves in hundreds fall upon his passing
While night sends down her dreadnought darkness
Upon this spurious Pentecost.

And the Melchisedec of our year's end
Who came without a parent, leaves without a trace,
And rain comes rattling down upon our forest
Like the doors of a country jail.

The Captives—A Psalm

Quomodo cantabimus canticum Domini in terra aliena?

Somewhere a king walks in his gallery
Owning the gorges of a fiery city.
Brass traffic shakes the walls. The windows shiver with
    business.
It is the bulls' day. The citizens

Build themselves each hour another god
And fry a fatter idol out of mud.

They cut themselves a crooked idiom
To the winged animals, upon their houses.
Prayers are made of money, songs of numbers,
Hymns of the blood of the killed.

Old ladies are treasured in sugar.
Young ones rot in wine.
The flesh of the fat organizers smiles with oil.

Blessed is the army that will one day crush you, city,
Like a golden spider.
Blest are they that hate you. Blest are they
That dash your brats against the stones.
The children of God have died, O Babylon,
Of thy wild algebra.

Days, days are the journey
From wall to wall. And miles
Miles of houses shelter terror.
And we lie chained to their dry roots, O Israel!

Our bodies are greyer than mud.
There, butterflies are born to be dancers
And fly in black and blue along the drunken river
Where, in the willow trees, Assyria lynched our song!

May my bones burn and ravens eat my flesh
If I forget thee, contemplation!
May language perish from my tongue
If I do not remember thee, O Sion, city of vision,
Whose heights have windows finer than the firmament
When night pours down her canticles
And peace sings on thy watchtowers like the stars of Job.

The City After Noon

What if the wild confinement were empty
And the felons were free to come home?
I saw Ohio, whom I love,
I saw the wide river between buildings
My big brown lady, going west.

What if the wild confinement were empty
And the policies were all gone!
If they could wash the stains of avarice
From faces, lust from the little houses,
And let some respiration through the satin sky!
What if the wild confinement were empty
And the lunatic pigeons were once again sane!

What a universe my tears betray
On St. Clare's Day, on St. Clare's Day!
Where the children of heaven are not yet born
And the fathers of destitution run
With horse, bottle and gun
To burn my river with their rum.
What a deluge my tears betray
On St. Clare's Day
When the Little One dies of hunger in His manger.
Is there none to entertain my daughter's stranger
Or take my old man's wager?
With horse, bottle and feathers
They have set fire to the most holy weather!

What if the wild contentment were full
And the furlongs were free to go farming!
I saw the river's daughters overwhelm a hill.
Water made all places plain.

There is a green wonder up and down Ohio:
Oh woods and woods, across my dangerous mother!
What if the wild contentment were full
And there were nothing left in the world
But fields, water and sun
And space went on forever to eternity, without a rim?

What if the wild confinement were empty
And the sheriffs were free to go home!

In the Rain and the Sun

Watch out for this peeled doorlight!
Here, without rain, without shame
My noonday dusk made spots upon the walk:
Tall drops pelted the concrete with their jewelry
Belonging to the old world's bones.

Owning this view, in the air of a hermit's weather,
I count the fragmentary rain
In drops as blue as coal
Until I plumb the shadows full of thunder.
My prayers supervise the atmosphere
Till storms call all hounds home.

Out of the towers of water
Four or five mountains come walking
To see the little monks' graves.
Flying the neutral stones I dwell between cedars
And see the countries sleeping in their beds:
Lands of the watermen, where poplars bend.

Wild seas amuse the world with water:
No end to all the surfs that charm our shores
Fattening the sands with their old foam and their old
    roar.

Thus in the boom of waves' advantage
Dogs and lions come to my tame home
Won by the bells of my Cistercian jungle.
O love the livid fringes
In which their robes are drenched!

Songs of the lions and whales!
With my pen between my fingers
Making the waterworld sing!
Sweet Christ, discover diamonds
And sapphires in my verse
While I burn the sap of my pine house
For praise of the ocean sun.

I have walked upon the whole days' surf
Rinsing Thy bays with hymns.
My eyes have swept horizons clean
Of ships and rain.
Upon the lacquered swells my feet no longer run.
Sliding all over the sea I come
To the hap of a slippery harbor.

Dogs have gone back to their ghosts
And the many lions, home.
But words fling wide the windows of their houses—
Adam and Eve walk down my coast
Praising the tears of the treasurer sun:
I hang Thy rubies on these autumn trees,
On the bones of the homegoing thunder.

Dry Places

No cars go by
Where dogs are barking at the desert.
Yet it is not twenty years since many lamps
Shed their juices in this one time town
And stores grew big lights, like oranges and pears.

Now not one lame miner
Sits on the rotten verandah,
Works in the irons where
Judas' shadow dwells.
Yet I could hew a city
From the side of their hill.

O deep stone covert where the dusk
Is full of lighted beasts
And the mad stars preach wars without end:
Whose bushes and grasses live without water,

There the skinny father of hate rolls in his dust
And if the wind should shift one leaf
The dead jump up and bark for their ghosts:
Their dry bones want our penniless souls.

Bones, go back to your baskets.
Get your fingers out of my clean skin.
Rest in your rainless death until your own souls
Come back in the appointed way and sort you out from
        your remains.

We who are still alive will wring a few green blades
From the floor of this valley
Though ploughs abhor your metal and your clay.

Rather than starve with you in rocks without oasis,
We will get up and work your loam
Until some prayer or some lean sentence
Bleeds like the quickest root they ever cut.

For we cannot forget the legend of the world's childhood
Or the track to the dogwood valley
And Adam our Father's old grass farm
Wherein they gave the animals names
And knew Christ was promised first without scars
When all God's larks called out to Him
In their wild orchard.

Je crois en l'Amour

Je crois en l'Amour
Qui dort et vit, caché dans les sémences,

Et lorsque je respire mon printemps
Dans la fraicheur des sommets liturgiques
En voyant tous les arbres et les blés verts,
L'émoi s'éveille au plus profond
De mon être mortel: et l'adoration
Sonne comme les cloches légendaires
Qui entonnent leurs chants sourds au sein de l'océan.

Et quand le soleil géant de mon été
A frappé l'or de toutes mes gerbes
Je fais fortune: c'est là mon chant, mon capital,
Ma louange de Notre Dame!

O frères, venez me rejoindre,
Buvez le vin de Melchisédec
Tandis que tous ces monts régenérés
Chantent la paix, vêtus des vignes d'Isaïe:

Car c'est ainsi que naissent les poëmes
Dans le creux de mon coeur d'homme
Et dans le sein de mon rocher fendu!

To the Immaculate Virgin, on a Winter Night

Lady, the night is falling and the dark
Steals all the blood from the scarred west.
The stars come out and freeze my heart
With drops of untouchable music, frail as ice
And bitter as the new year's cross.

Where in the world has any voice
Prayed to you, Lady, for the peace that's in your power?
In a day of blood and many beatings
I see the governments rise up, behind the steel horizon,
And take their weapons and begin to kill.

Where in the world has any city trusted you?
Out where the soldiers camp the guns begin to thump
And another winter time comes down

To seal our years in ice.
The last train cries out
And runs in terror from this farmers' valley
Where all the little birds are dead.

The roads are white, the fields are mute
There are no voices in the wood
And trees make gallows up against the sharp-eyed stars.
Oh where will Christ be killed again
In the land of these dead men?

Lady, the night has got us by the heart
And the whole world is tumbling down.
Words turn to ice in my dry throat
Praying for a land without prayer,

Walking to you on water all winter
In a year that wants more war.

A Responsory, 1948

Suppose the dead could crown their wit
With some intemperate exercise,
Spring wine from their ivory
Or roses from their eyes?

Or if the wise could understand
And the world without heart
That the dead are not yet dead
And that the living live apart

And the wounded are healing,
Though in a place of flame.
The sick in a great ship
Are riding. They are riding home.

Suppose the dead could crown their wit
With some intemperate exercise,
Spring wine from their ivory
Or roses from their eyes?

Two cities sailed together
For many thousand years.
And now they drift asunder.
The tides of new wars

Sweep the sad heavens,
Divide the massed stars,
The black and white universe
The booming spheres.

Down, down, down
The white armies fall
Moving their ordered snows
Toward the jaws of hell.

Suppose the dead could crown their wit
With some intemperate exercise,
Spring wine from their ivory
Or roses from their eyes?

A Psalm

When psalms surprise me with their music
And antiphons turn to rum
The Spirit sings: the bottom drops out of my soul

And from the center of my cellar, Love, louder than
      thunder
Opens a heaven of naked air.

New eyes awaken.
I send Love's name into the world with wings
And songs grow up around me like a jungle.
Choirs of all creatures sing the tunes
Your Spirit played in Eden.
Zebras and antelopes and birds of paradise
Shine on the face of the abyss
And I am drunk with the great wilderness
Of the sixth day in Genesis.

But sound is never half so fair
As when that music turns to air
And the universe dies of excellence.

Sun, moon and stars
Fall from their heavenly towers.
Joys walk no longer down the blue world's shore.

Though fires loiter, lights still fly on the air of the gulf,
All fear another wind, another thunder:
Then one more voice
Snuffs all their flares in one gust.

And I go forth with no more wine and no more stars
And no more buds and no more Eden
And no more animals and no more sea:
While God sings by Himself in acres of night
And walls fall down, that guarded Paradise.

Senescente Mundo

Senescente mundo, when the hot globe
Shrivels and cracks
And uninhibited atoms resolve
Earth and water, fruit and flower, body and animal soul,
All the blue stars come tumbling down.
Beauty and ugliness and love and hate
Wisdom and politics are all alike undone.

Toward that fiery day we run like crabs
With our bad-tempered armor on.
"With blood and carpets, oranges and ashes,
Rubber and limes and bones,"
(So sing the children on the Avenue)
"With cardboard and dirty water and a few flames for
        the Peacelover's ghost,
We know where the dead bodies are
Studying the ceiling from the floors of their homes,
With smoke and roses, slate and wire
And crushed fruit and much fire."

Yet in the middle of this murderous season
Great Christ, my fingers touch Thy wheat
And hold Thee hidden in the compass of Thy paper sun.
There is no war will not obey this cup of Blood,
This wine in which I sink Thy words, in the anonymous
    dawn!
I hear a Sovereign talking in my arteries
Reversing, with His Promises, all things
That now go on with fire and thunder.
His Truth is greater than disaster.
His Peace imposes silence on the evidence against us.

And though the world, at last, has swallowed her own
    solemn laughter
And has condemned herself to hell:
Suppose a whole new universe, a great clean Kingdom
Were to rise up like an Atlantis in the East,
Surprise this earth, this cinder, with new holiness!

Here in my hands I hold that secret Easter.
Tomorrow, this will be my Mass's answer,
Because of my companions whom the wilderness has
    eaten,
Crying like Jonas in the belly of our whale.